PRIMARY EXPLORERS

HUMAN BODY

Author:
Kirsty Neale

igloobooks

CONTENTS

YOUR BRILLIANT BODY

The human body is an amazing and complicated place, both inside and out.

It works like a powerful machine, with bones, muscles, nerves, organs and tissues all helping to keep us alive. The fuel that keeps our body going comes from food, water and oxygen in the air we breathe. Without these things, our bodies can't work properly and we quickly become ill.

WHAT ARE YOU DOING?

Each part of our body has its own particular job, from muscles that help us walk, blink, chew and play sports, to organs that let us sing, or watch TV. Even when we're asleep, our body is busy breathing, growing and repairing itself. Many parts of the body work together in groups, so we can do clever and more complicated things. Right now, for example, you're using your muscles to hold this book, your eyes to read the words and your brain to understand the words.

The bones that make up the skeleton are tough and hard-working. They support and protect the rest of the body.

MADE OF WATER

More than half of our body is made up of water, but some of it is lost every time we breathe, sweat, or go to the toilet. It's important to replace the lost water by drinking lots every day.

DID YOU KNOW?

The human body has more than 20 internal organs, including the heart, brain, lungs and liver. Most of them are found in the abdomen (between the chest and hips).

PARTS OF THE BODY

People come in all shapes and sizes. Some are tall and skinny, others are short and round. Different races may have dark, or fair skin, straight, or curly hair, blue, or brown eyes. We can have big teeth, squashy noses, long fingers, or little ears. But, even though we look different, everyone has the same body parts and features.

Under the skin are sheets of muscles. They're made up of light and dark strands and are sometimes called striated, which means stripy!

The soft part of the body between our skin and bones is called flesh. It's made up of fat, tissue and muscles.

DID YOU KNOW?

Scientists who study the structure of human bodies are called anatomists. They learn by examining skeletons and real people, as well as from books.

THE SKELETON

The human body is held together by a strong framework of bones, called the skeleton.

The skeleton supports our muscles and protects our organs. More than a dozen bones protect our brain and 12 pairs of ribs form a cage around our heart and lungs. As well as protecting our organs, the skeleton plays an important part in allowing us to move. The bones form levers, which muscles pull to move different parts of the body.

DID YOU KNOW?

A baby's skeleton has more than 300 bones, but an adult has only 206. This is because some of the bones fuse together as the body grows.

Skull

Forehead

Upper jaw

Lower jaw

JOINTS

A moveable joint is where two or more bones 'join' together, but do not actually touch. They allow the skeleton to move.

Hinge
(knees and elbows)

Ball and socket
(hips and shoulders)

Gliding
(wrists and ankles)

Saddle
(thumbs)

The lower jaw bone holds the lower teeth in place. It's the biggest, strongest bone in the face and the only large bone in the skull that can move.

Skull

Shoulder-blade

Rib

Vertebrae of spine (backbone)

Wrist bones

The only saddle joint in the body is in the thumbs. It allows the thumbs to move back and forth and from side to side (with limited rotation).

A ball and socket joint, such as the shoulder joint, allows one bone to rotate at almost any angle to the other bone.

Breastbone

Hipbone (pelvis)

Fingerbone

The knee is a hinge joint. It works like a door hinge, allowing us to swing our lower leg forwards and backwards.

Thighbone

Calfbone

Shinbone

Anklebone

THE SPINE

Our spine, or backbone, allows us to bend, twist and stand upright. It supports our head and helps us keep our balance as we move around. Rather than being a single, long bone, it's made up of 33 separate bones, called vertebrae. These are shaped like rings and together, they protect the delicate spinal cord.

Toebone

Kneecap

Your ankles and wrists have gliding joints. These allow the bones to slide past each other.

BONES AND CELLS

The bones that make up the skeleton are strong, lightweight and full of living cells.

Cells are sometimes called the building blocks of life. They are the smallest living things on Earth and, when joined together, make up all larger living things – plants, animals and humans. Each part of your body is made from millions of cells. They come in different shapes and sizes and all have their own special job to do.

When you see a real skeleton, or bones in a museum, they look dry, crumbly and dead. But the living bones inside your body are very different. They're busy growing and changing, just like the rest of you.

CLEVER CARTILAGE

When you're born, some of your bones are made of a firm, but flexible material called cartilage. As you get older and grow, most of the cartilage becomes hard and turns into bone. Some of it stays soft though, and can be found in joints, where it stops two bones from rubbing together. You can also feel small amounts of soft cartilage at the top of your ears and at the tip of your nose.

Cell divides into two

Cluster of cells

Some of the cells in the body don't live for very long. When they die, the rest of the cells need to replace them. To do this, they divide or split themselves in half, so one old cell becomes two new cells. The two new cells then divide to become a cluster of cells.

Tendons join muscle to bone

The calf muscle is a skeletal muscle. When the muscle squeezes, it becomes shorter. This pulls the bones closer together and forces the joints to bend.

Thread-like part of muscle

Connecting tissue

Ligaments join bone to bone

Muscles are attached to bones by bands of strong, stretchy tissue called tendons. These are similar to ligaments, which join one bone to another, and fascia, which connect different muscles together.

Bone

The cells in a muscle are arranged in tube-shaped bundles. They slide smoothly past each other when we squeeze and relax our muscles.

BONE MARROW

Inside the hard, outer layer of many bones is a hollow space that helps to keep the skeleton light. It contains a soft, jelly-like material called bone marrow. A small amount of the bone marrow is yellow, and contains fat cells, but most of it is red. The red bone marrow makes blood cells, which carry oxygen all around the body and also help us to fight germs and disease.

FAT CELLS

When we eat, our body turns the food into energy. If we don't use all the food-energy straight away, it is stored in special fat cells called lipocytes.

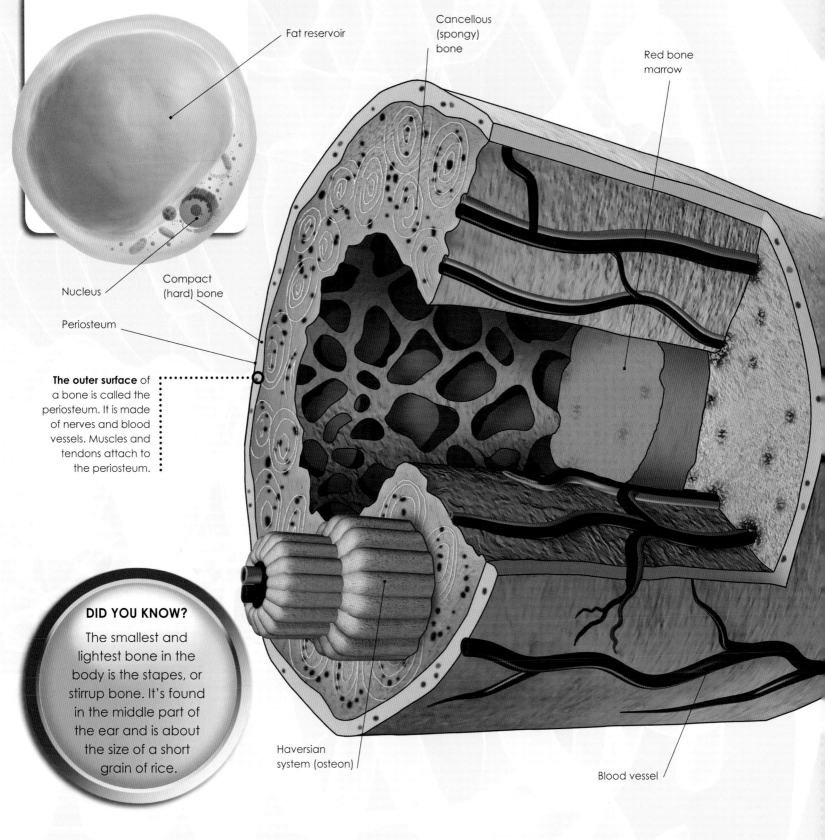

Fat reservoir

Nucleus

Compact (hard) bone

Periosteum

The outer surface of a bone is called the periosteum. It is made of nerves and blood vessels. Muscles and tendons attach to the periosteum.

Cancellous (spongy) bone

Red bone marrow

Haversian system (osteon)

Blood vessel

DID YOU KNOW?

The smallest and lightest bone in the body is the stapes, or stirrup bone. It's found in the middle part of the ear and is about the size of a short grain of rice.

MUSCLES AND MOVING

Life would be a lot less fun without muscles!

Every time we move, it's our muscles that are doing the work. We couldn't walk, talk, play games, or eat anything without them. They also take care of other important actions, such as blinking and breathing.

The muscles that help our arms and legs to bend are called flexors. The muscles that straighten them out again are called extensors. Biceps are flexors and triceps are extensors.

PULLING PAIRS

There are over 630 muscles in the body and they make up nearly half our body weight. Many of them work in groups. This is partly because muscles can only pull, they can't push. By working in pairs, two muscles can pull in opposite directions and that allows us to move parts of our body in different directions, too.

There are over 30 muscles in the face

FACE MUSCLES

Some of the muscles in the face are attached to skin, instead of bone. They help us to smile, frown, wink, raise our eyebrows, or show how we're feeling. Eye muscles are the body's busiest muscles, moving about 100,000 times each day!

Muscles let us express emotions

When we're worried, the muscles in the head sometimes squeeze together too hard. If this keeps happening, they become tired and painful, causing the most common kind of headache.

Pectorals

Deltoids

Biceps

Abdominals

Gastrocnemius

Quadriceps femoris

MUSCLE TYPES

There are three different types of muscle in the body. Smooth muscle helps internal organs, such as the lungs and stomach, to work properly. Cardiac muscle is found only in the heart and its job is to keep the heart beating. Skeletal muscles are the most common muscles. They are attached to bones and they help us move around. They're also known as voluntary muscles, because we can control how and when we want them to work.

Hand muscles can make big, simple movements, such as grabbing. They can also make small, precise movements that allow us to do complicated tasks, such as drawing, or fastening buttons.

DID YOU KNOW?

Muscles help to keep us warm. Every time we move, the muscles in the body give off heat. The body uses this heat to keep us at the right temperature.

A heartbeat, also known as the cardiac cycle, has four stages.

1 First, the heart relaxes and blood enters through the veins.

2 Then the atria contract, or squeeze, and force blood into the ventricles.

3 Next the ventricles contract and the blood is squeezed hard.

4 Finally, the blood is forced out through valves into the main arteries.

THE HEART

The heart is one of the most important organs in the body.

About the same size as a fist, it's actually a muscle. It sits in the middle of the chest, protected by the ribcage and beats all the time, even when we're asleep.

PUMPING BLOOD

The heart's main job is to pump blood around the body, delivering the oxygen it needs to keep working. The blood comes in through veins on the right side of the heart and is pumped out into the lungs. There, it's mixed with oxygen, which comes from the air we breathe. From the lungs, the blood goes into the left side of the heart, where it's pumped back out into the body.

YOUR BEATING HEART

When you feel your heart beating, it's actually the squeezing and relaxing of the heart muscle that you can feel. Inside the heart, four valves open and close to allow the movement of blood. The regular 'thud' of your heartbeat is made by the valves as they close.

The heart is divided into four separate areas, or chambers. The two at the top are called atria (the left atrium and right atrium) and the two below are ventricles.

DID YOU KNOW?

People used to think that feelings came from the heart, but it's really the brain that controls how fast the heart beats when a person is feeling happy, sad, or scared.

TAKING A PULSE

Doctors 'take' or measure a pulse to find out if a patient's heart is beating too fast, or too slow. One way to do this is to press two fingers against the artery in the wrist and count the number of heartbeats, or pulses, you can feel the heart make in one minute. Each beat is a blood pressure bulge from the heart that is carried along the artery.

Aorta and main
arteries to body

Pulmonary valve

Pulmonary artery (to lungs)

Left atrium

Aortic
valve

Right
atrium

Mitral
valve

THE FOUR VALVES

The valves inside the
heart connect the
four chambers. They
work like one-way
doors to keep
blood flowing in the
right direction. The
valves open to let
blood go through,
then close to stop it
flowing backwards. The
mitral and tricuspid valves
let blood flow from the
atria to the ventricles. The
aortic and pulmonary
valves control blood
leaving the heart.

DID YOU KNOW?

The average person's
heart beats more than
30 million times in just
one year. During that
time, it pumps about
3.3 million litres (730,000
gallons) of blood
around the body.

Right
ventricle

Tricuspid
valve

Tendons
(heartstrings)

Left ventricle

Blood is made up of red cells, white cells and platelets floating in a watery, yellow liquid, called plasma. A single drop of blood contains over 5 million cells.

Red blood cells carry oxygen. They live for about 120 days.

White blood cells help defend the body against illness. They attack and destroy any germs that enter the body.

Platelets are cells that repair broken blood vessels. They stick together, or clot, when you cut yourself to stop the bleeding.

BLOOD, VEINS AND ARTERIES

Together, veins and arteries are known as blood vessels.

Blood travels through tube-shaped blood vessels to reach cells all over the body. It delivers oxygen and takes away waste, keeping the cells and body healthy.

RED AND BLUE

The blood in our veins is a darker shade of red than the blood in our arteries. This is because it contains less oxygen. So, why do the veins under the surface of the skin look blue? Veins are actually white, but the effect of dark red blood flowing through them and skin on top, makes them appear blue.

Arteries are like hoses with thick, stretchy walls. They carry blood away from the heart. Veins are usually thinner. They take blood and waste back towards the heart.

Heart

Blood vessel

The cardiovascular system is made up of our heart, blood and blood vessels. It works so efficiently that each blood cell takes just twenty seconds to circle the whole body.

ON THE ATTACK

Sometimes the body catches a virus – a germ that causes a disease such as measles, or chickenpox. When this happens, the body produces extra white blood cells, shown here with red blood cells, to fight off the virus and stop us getting ill.

DID YOU KNOW?
Red blood cells are shaped a bit like doughnuts. This gives them a bigger surface area than flat, or ball-shaped cells, which means they can carry even more oxygen around the body.

BLOOD GROUPS

Everyone's blood belongs to a particular blood group, or type, depending on which special markers the blood has on the surface of the red blood cells. There are about thirty different groups, including A, B, O and AB. If a person loses a lot of blood through an injury, or during an operation, they may need to have their own blood topped up with someone else's blood. This process is called a blood transfusion.

Arteries and veins take blood to and from every part of the body, even the ends of our toes. The whole blood vessel system is so big that if you stretched it out, it could wrap twice around the Earth.

TAKING A BREATH

Lungs allow our body to take in fresh air and get rid of stale air.

Fresh air contains oxygen and lungs work with the cardiovascular system to send it all around the body. Stale air is then brought back to the lungs and expelled as we breathe out.

The body is brilliant at making sure our lungs and airways are kept clear, so we can breathe easily.

When we cough, it's usually because there's something in our lungs which shouldn't be there, such as dust, smoke, or an infection. Coughing forces air out of the lungs, as the body tries to get rid of the irritation.

A sneeze happens if something irritates our nose. The lungs force air out in a sneeze, instead of a cough.

Hiccups happen when our diaphragm is over-working. Extra air rushes into the lungs and as it hits the voicebox – hic!

TAKE A BREATH

Our lungs take up almost all of the space in our chest. They work together with a large muscle called the diaphragm, which sits underneath the ribcage. When we breathe in, air goes down through our windpipe into two big tubes, known as bronchi. Each bronchi branches off inside the lungs into more tubes, which gradually get smaller. The thinnest tubes are called bronchioli and each one leads into a tiny air sac, or alveolus.

Alveolus

Inside each of our lungs we have about 300 million alveoli, or air sacs. Every time we take a breath, the alveoli fill with air, making our lungs expand like a balloon.

BREATHING IN AND OUT

When you breathe in, your diaphragm squashes itself flat and your ribs lift upwards. This gives your lungs room to inflate. When you breathe out again, your diaphragm relaxes, your ribs move down and the air is pushed back out.

Air in

Air out

Nasal
passage

Voicebox
(larynx)

Windpipe
(trachea)

Right lung

Left lung

Nose

Mouth

Epiglottis

The mouth, nose and windpipe warm up the air
we breathe in and add moisture. The epiglottis
prevents food from entering the windpipe.

THE IMPORTANCE OF PLANTS

Plants are an important part of every single breath
we take. The human body takes in oxygen, uses
it up and then breathes out the waste gas,
carbon dioxide. Plants, including trees,
flowers and grass, do the opposite.
They take in carbon dioxide,
use it up and give out
oxygen. So, without
plants, we'd have
no 'fresh air'
and without
us, neither
would they!

Bronchus

Bronchiole

Alveoli

Diaphragm

DID YOU KNOW?

To make room for the
heart, your left lung is
smaller than your right.
Between the two of them,
the surface area of your
lungs could cover half a
tennis court!

THE BRAIN

Inside our skull is an amazing, complicated and powerful super-computer.

Our brain is in charge of almost everything that goes on in the rest of the body. It controls muscles, organs, senses, the way we feel and is also home to all the things we know and remember.

MIND MATTERS

It might not look very impressive, but the lumpy, walnut-shaped human brain is so complicated that scientists still don't know everything about the way it works. It has evolved over millions of years and is made up of billions of cells. To work in the most efficient way, the brain is divided into different areas. Some parts are used for storing memories, some parts help us to learn and solve problems, some parts control groups of muscles and other parts are in charge of speech.

Emotions, such as sadness, or joy, are often said to come from the heart, but they actually come from the brain. Scientists have discovered that two almond-shaped groups of cells called the amygdala are the part of the brain involved in feelings.

When the brain recognizes an emotion, it sends signals telling the rest of the body how to act. Happy feelings can curve our lips into a smile, while feelings of anger might make us frown, or shout.

LEFT AND RIGHT SIDES OF THE BRAIN

Left hemisphere

Right hemisphere

The brain is divided into two sides, or hemispheres. The left side of the brain controls the right side of the body and the right side of the brain controls the left side of the body. A big fold divides the two parts of the brain, but they are connected by a thick bundle of nerves at the base of the brain.

PARTS OF THE BRAIN

Over three-quarters of the brain is made up of the cerebrum. This is the part we use for thinking, remembering and solving problems. It also controls our voluntary muscles. The cerebellum is much smaller. It takes care of balance and coordination. Each of these brain parts is joined to the spinal cord by the brain stem. The stem looks after our involuntary muscles and controls things such as breathing and heartbeat.

Cerebrospinal fluid in the space around the brain helps to keep germs away from the brain and cushions it if the head gets knocked

Cerebrum

Skull (cranium)

Visual cortex (controls seeing)

Thalamus (relay station for most information going into the brain)

Amygdala (involved in feelings, especially fear)

Pons (nerve highway)

Cerebellum (coordinates movement)

Brain stem

Spinal cord

The brain and body communicate using special nerve messages. These are sorted by the brain stem, which delivers them to exactly the right part of the brain, or body.

DID YOU KNOW?

If you could smooth out all the wrinkles and folds in your brain to spread it flat, it would cover an area about three times bigger than your whole head!

THE NERVOUS SYSTEM

The nerves, brain and spinal cord make up the nervous system. They work together to send messages around the whole body.

The nerves gather information – maybe from something felt, or touched – and pass it along the spinal cord to the brain. The brain then sends messages back out so the body can act on the information.

WHAT ARE NERVES?

The nervous system contains billions of tiny nerve cells called neurons. Each individual nerve is like a thread, made up of neurons bundled together. The biggest nerves are over 2 cm (0.8 in) thick and the smallest are thinner than a human hair. There are two main types of neuron in the body – sensory neurons and motor neurons. Sensory neurons send messages to the brain about the outside world, and how we're feeling. Motor neurons pass information from the brain to the muscles.

When a neuron is excited, either by the senses, or by chemicals in the body, it gives off a small spark of electricity called a nerve impulse. These nerve impulses 'jump' from one neuron to the next across a small gap called a synapse.

Central nervous system (brain and spinal cord)

DID YOU KNOW?

Nerves don't just act on messages from external senses (sight, sound, hearing, touch and taste). They also take care of senses inside the body, such as hunger and thirst.

NETWORK OF NERVES

The nervous system has two main parts – the central nervous system, made up of the brain and spinal cord, and the peripheral nervous system, made up of nerves passing to all parts of the body. If someone has an injury and their nerves become damaged, they may feel pain, numbness, or even paralysis (their muscles stop working).

Peripheral nervous system (nerves)

Brain

We have more
pain-sensing neurons
than any other type.
They're found in the
joints, organs, skin and
bones. If any part of
the body is damaged,
they send pain signals
to the brain.

The spinal cord is a long,
tube-shaped bundle of
nerves. It sits inside the spinal
column and is protected by
tough vertebrae all the way
around. As nerves branch
off from the spinal cord, they
divide many times to reach
every part of the body.

Spinal cord

Spinal column

Vertebra

Nerve

LOOKING AT EYES

Eyes let the body take in all sorts of information about the outside world.

Our eyes are well protected. They sit inside deep sockets under a tough brow bone. But this is only the start of the clever protection system.

Our eyelids shut quickly if anything threatens our eyes, or comes too close to the eyeballs. They also protect against very bright light.

Eyelashes grow above and below the eye. They trap specks of dust and dirt and keep them out of our eyes.

Eyebrows stop sweat and other types of moisture from running off our forehead and into our eyes.

Wherever we are, whatever we're doing, our eyes are busy collecting images to send to the brain. As well as seeing every shade of the rainbow, they also see light, movement and shapes, helping us make sense of our surroundings.

PARTS OF THE EYE

The clear, glassy dome at the front of the eye is called the cornea. It sits on top of the blue, brown, or green iris. In the middle of each eye, the black pupil is actually an opening in the iris. It shrinks and expands to control how much light enters the eye.

INSIDE THE EYE

Behind the pupil is a clear lens. It focuses light onto the retina at the back of the eye. Special cells in the retina, called rods, turn the light into a shaded image. More cells, called cones, work out if the image is yellow, green, violet, or another shade. The eye then sends the picture it sees along the optic nerve to the brain.

IT'S OK TO CRY!

Every time we blink, our eye produces tears. The eyelids wash the tears over the eyeballs to stop them drying out and to rinse away any specks of dust, or dirt.

Tears

The image on the retina is upside down, but the brain translates the picture so we 'see' it the right way up.

Upside-down image on retina

Rays of light

Object

Lens

Optic nerve

SPECTACULAR MUSCLES!

The lenses in our eyes use muscles to focus, or get a clear picture. As the muscles squeeze and relax, they change the shape of the lens, allowing us to see things nearby, or far away. Some people have lenses that don't focus properly. Pictures fall too far in front of, or behind the retina and look blurry. To fix this problem, people wear glasses.

Muscles

Lens

Retina

The eyeball is about 25 mm (1 inch) across. Six muscles attach the eyeball to the bones of the socket behind the eye.

Sclera

Iris

Cornea

Pupil

Vitreous gel, a clear jelly-like material that fills the space between the lens and the retina

DID YOU KNOW?

Most people blink 10 to 15 times a minute. Eyes stay closed for 0.35 seconds with each blink. Our eyes are shut for over half an hour a day, just through blinking!

Hear, hear!

Ears aren't just for listening and hearing, they also help us keep our balance.

These clever organs collect sounds and pass them to the brain, which makes sense of them.

Outer ear (auricle)

Feeling dizzy and losing our balance are sensations created partly in our ears. Above the cochlea are three tubes, called semicircular canals, containing liquid and hair-covered cells. When our head moves, the liquid moves, too. The cells send signals to the brain, which adjusts our balance. If we spin round very quickly, the signals can get confused and make us feel dizzy.

Sometimes our ears pop! This happens when the air pressure inside our ears changes, for example, when we enter a tunnel at high speed. To balance this out, some of the air escapes along a special tube, called the Eustachian tube. The 'pop' happens when the tube opens and the air is released.

HOW DO WE HEAR?

When something makes a noise, it sends vibrations, known as sound waves, through the air. The vibrations reach the outer ear, which funnels them through the ear canal to the eardrum. When they reach the eardrum, it vibrates and starts a chain reaction, sending the vibrations to the middle ear and then the inner ear.

GETTING THE MESSAGE

In the inner ear is a shell-shaped part called the cochlea. The cochlea is filled with liquid and lined with cells covered in tiny hairs. As the liquid vibrates, it moves the hairs. The hairs then send nerve signals to the brain, which translates the vibrations into sound messages.

HEARING LOSS

Deafness and loss of hearing have many different causes. People can be born completely deaf, or become hard of hearing later in life. Some people who can't hear normal speech use sign language to communicate instead.

In American sign language, this symbol means 'I love you.'

WONDERFUL WAX

Our body produces earwax to keep our ears clean and well-protected. It's made by glands in the ear canal. As well as stopping the skin in our ears from getting dry and itchy, it keeps out dust, dirt and even small insects!

Ears can become blocked by earwax. A doctor can check this by shining a bright light into our ears to see inside.

Semicircular canal

Anvil (incus)

Nerve
(attaches to
auditory nerve)

Hammer
(malleus)

Stirrup

Cochlea

Middle ear

Inner ear

Eardrum (a thin
piece of tightly-
stretched skin)

Eustachian
tube

Ear canal
(about 2.5 cm/1 inch long)

The stirrup, or stapes, is
the smallest bone in the
body. It is one of three
tiny bones, called ossicles,
that vibrate in the middle
ear. The other two are the
hammer and anvil.

Ear lobe

HOW DO WE SMELL?

Our nose can sniff out all kinds of things, from danger to tasty snacks.

It might seem less important than seeing and hearing, but our sense of smell is every bit as vital to the way we live and enjoy our life.

SMELL THAT!
Smells are made up of tiny scent particles in the air. When we sniff, they flow into the cavity behind the nose. The upper lining of the nasal cavity contains millions of cells that recognize different scent particles. When they sense a particular smell, a signal is sent to the brain.

SMELL AND THE BRAIN
The olfactory cortex is the part of the brain that sorts out smells. It communicates with other parts of the brain to work out exactly what we can smell. If it's something that could be dangerous, such as fire, our brain prepares the rest of our body to act, too.

When we catch a cold, the virus that causes it makes itself at home in our nasal cavity. The sensitive lining of the nose swells up and becomes irritated, making us sneeze more than usual. Cold germs are easily spread by the droplets that we sneeze out. There are around 40,000 of them in just a single sneeze.

Virus

DID YOU KNOW?
Our sense of smell helps us taste food better. Try putting it to the test – block out smells by pinching your nose, then eat a mouthful of food and see how it tastes.

Our sense of smell is closely linked to memory. The brain uses this link and always connects new smells to a particular memory.

Sometimes people sneeze when they look at a bright light. Doctors think this happens because of a mix-up in the signals sent between the eyes, nose and brain.

SNEEZING
When we sneeze, it's usually because something has tickled or irritated the inside of our nose. Our body goes through an incredible process, just to get rid of what might be a few tiny particles of dust. The tickle in the nose sends a message to the brain, which then sends its own message to muscles in the stomach, chest, throat and face. The muscles work together in exactly the right order to form a sneeze and blast the ticklish particles out of the nose. It's difficult to measure, but experts think that a sneeze travels at between 80 and 160 km per hour (50 and 100 miles per hour) as it leaves the nose.

The nostrils are the two holes at the end of the nose. They are divided by a wall, called the septum. You can feel through your skin that the top of your nose is made of thin bone and the end is soft cartilage.

The olfactory bulb is just above the nasal cavity, underneath the front of the brain. This is connected to the brain by the olfactory nerve.

Olfactory cells

Tooth

Nasal cavity

Lip

Hard palate

Tongue

DID YOU KNOW?

A human nose is much less sensitive than a dog's nose. We have around 10 million smell-detecting cells in our nose, but a dog has more than 200 million!

MEGA MOUTHS

We can do all sorts of wonderful things with our mouth – taste, talk, sing, whistle and even kiss!

The mouth works together with the teeth and tongue so we can chew and swallow food. Teamed with our lungs, it also lets us make sounds, from the quietest whisper to screams and shouts.

Lips are covered with a very thin layer of skin – thinner than on the rest of the face. This means that the blood vessels underneath show through more easily, so our lips look dark pink or, in cold weather, when blood flow is slower, purple-ish blue.

We often have to purse our lips to make certain words and sounds. We also have to purse our lips to whistle.

SPIT IT OUT!

Saliva, or spit, plays an important part in keeping the mouth healthy. Without it, the tongue would very quickly dry out and our tastebuds would stop working. The chemicals in saliva help to keep the mouth naturally clean and free from germs. It also works with the tongue and teeth to break down food, ready for us to swallow.

SAY HELLO

Our voicebox, or larynx, is in the throat. As we breathe, air goes through the larynx and over two small folds, called vocal chords. Muscles in the larynx squeeze the vocal chords together when we speak and the air causes them to vibrate. The mouth makes the noise louder, like a speaker, and the teeth and tongue shape the sounds into words.

DID YOU KNOW?

The tongue is mostly made up of strong skeletal muscles, and is home to about 10,000 tastebuds. Just like fingerprints, everyone's tongue-print is unique!

The muscles in and around the lips help us eat, whistle, smile, sip drinks through a straw and form letters such as 'p' and 'w' when we talk.

TASTEBUDS

Tastebuds are clumps of cells all over the surface of the tongue that act like tiny sensors. They send messages to the brain, which then works out what we are tasting. The five basic types of taste are sweet, salty, sour, bitter and savory (umami).

Sweet

Salty

Savory (umami)

Sour

Bitter

The surface of the tongue is covered in tiny bumps, called papillae. These hold and move food around as we chew. They also contain the tastebuds.

Uvula

Upper lip

Tonsil

Lower lip

Tongue

The tonsils and uvula are at the back of the mouth. Tonsils help the body fight off infections and the uvula stops us choking on our food.

Hair, Nails and Teeth

Some of the most obvious signs that we're growing and changing come from our hair, nails and teeth.

Hair gets its shade of black, brown, or red from a chemical called melanin. The amount of melanin controls the exact shade of the hair. Blonde and red-headed people have less melanin than those with brown, or black hair.

Almost every part of the outside of the body is covered in hair. Some of it is easy to see, especially on the head, but in other places, the hair is so fine it's nearly invisible.

Baby-teeth fall out from about the age of five and are slowly replaced with a set of bigger teeth. Nails and hair are constantly being replaced.

HAIR GROWTH

A head is covered with about 100,000 hairs and each strand starts from a root. It's fed by tiny blood vessels until it grows up and out through the skin. The hair keeps growing for two to six years until, eventually, it falls out. It's then replaced by a brand new hair.

The root of a hair grows under the surface of the skin in a tiny, tube-shaped group of cells called a follicle.

Oil from glands below the follicles helps to protect hair and make it look glossy.

Straight hair grows from straight follicles, while people with curly hair have follicles that are hooked at the end.

Nail body   Nail bed   Cuticle

Fingernails grow 2 to 3 mm (0.08 to 0.1 in) per month. Toenails grow more slowly.

Root

NAILS

Nails are made from the same material as hair. It's called keratin and is the perfect tough surface to protect our fingertips and toes. Each nail grows from a root, hidden under the skin and protected by cuticles. As new nail cells develop, they push the old ones out. Once above the skin, the old cells harden and form what we think of as nails.

The pulp in a tooth contains nerve-endings and blood vessels. It's the part that hurts when you have toothache.

Crown   Dentin   Pulp   Root

TEETH

Teeth help us chew food and pronounce certain sounds when we talk. The hard, white outside layer is made from enamel. It protects the dentin, the pulp and the root, which fixes the tooth to the jawbone.

X-ray of a tooth and its roots

Incisors

Canines

Premolars

Molars

Your mouth contains four different kinds of teeth. Incisors are sharp and chisel-shaped, for biting. Pointed canine teeth tear off pieces of food for the premolars to crush and chew. Lastly, strong molars grind the food, ready to be swallowed.

FOOD IS FUEL

Food provides our body with the energy it needs to work, grow and stay healthy.

The digestive system takes nutrients, including vitamins and minerals, out of the food we eat and puts them to work all around the body.

DID YOU KNOW?

If your small intestine was unfolded and stretched out, it would measure more than 6.7 m (20 feet) long. Food takes roughly four hours to travel from one end to the other.

READY, SET, GO!

The digestive system actually gets to work at the first tempting whiff of food! As you breathe in the smell of the food, saliva forms in the mouth. Once you take a bite and start chewing, chemicals in the saliva get to work breaking down the food. It forms a soft ball and your tongue pushes it to the back of your throat. As you swallow, it drops into your oesophagus, a stretchy pipe also known as the gullet. Muscles in the walls of the oesophagus move the food down into the stomach.

The stomach is lined with strong muscles that mash up food. It also releases chemicals that soften the food into a liquid.

The kidneys filter out waste products in the bloodstream to keep it clean and healthy. They then produce urine to get rid of the waste.

THE INTESTINES

From your stomach, food moves into the small intestine. Here, all the nutrients are taken out of the food. The nutrients flow into your bloodstream and the leftover food goes through to your large intestine. Two organs, the liver and the pancreas, produce digestive juices that help break down the food. The juices enter the small intestine through small tubes called ducts.

Stomach

Small intestine

Large intestine

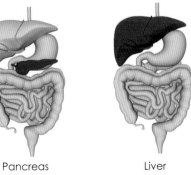
Pancreas

Liver

Oesophagus

The liver produces a digestive juice called bile, which is stored between meals in the gallbladder. When bile enters the small intestine, it dissolves the fat in food.

Gallbladder

Stomach

Spleen

Kidney

Small intestine

Large intestine

Body temperature is controlled by blood vessels, hair, sweat glands and skin. If you're too hot, blood vessels widen to increase the blood flow and you begin to sweat. This releases heat from inside the body and as sweat evaporates, it also cools the skin.

Hot and sweaty

When you're cold, blood vessels shrink to keep warm blood away from the chilly surface of your skin. Tiny hairs on the skin stand up to trap heat. This also puckers the skin, causing goosebumps.

Feeling cold

AMAZING SKIN

Strong and stretchy, the skin is the body's protective cover and largest organ.

As well as holding bones, muscles and organs inside, our skin also keeps out germs. It allows us to touch and feel and even repairs itself when damaged.

NEW SKIN

Skin has two main layers. In the lower layer, or dermis, there are nerve-endings, blood vessels and glands. The upper layer, or epidermis, is where new skin cells are made. Once the cells are ready, they rise to the top of the epidermis and take the place of older, dead cells. The dead cells fall off. We shed millions of them every day, but there are always new cells waiting to replace them.

Some of the cells in our skin make a chemical called melanin. This is what makes the skin dark or light. Dark-skinned people have more melanin than those with fair skin.

Hair shaft

Epidermis

Sweat pore

Dermis

Sweat gland

MOLES

Melanocytes are the cells in the skin that make melanin. When they gather together in tightly-packed groups, they form moles. These are small brown, or tan spots on the skin. They are usually round, or oval in shape. Moles are more common in people with fair skin.

Nerve ending

Freckles are small patches of concentrated melanin. Skin makes extra melanin to protect itself from the sun, which is why freckles appear darker in summer.

Sebaceous (oil) gland

DID YOU KNOW?

On average, an area of skin the size of a stamp has 30,000 melanin-producing cells, 300 sweat glands, 2,000 oil glands, 10 blood vessels and over 500 nerve endings.

Hair follicle

Under the surface of the skin, sebaceous glands make a kind of waxy oil. This keeps skin soft and also makes it naturally waterproof.

Hypodermis (fatty tissue)

WRINKLES

As we get older, our skin doesn't make as many new cells. It gets thinner and starts to dry out. It also loses some of its stretchiness. Together, these things cause skin to droop and fold into wrinkles.

Deep wrinkles

HOW WE BEGIN

Long strands of genes are known as chromosomes. Each of our cells has 46 chromosomes – 23 from our mother and 23 from our father.

Chromosomes

Egg and sperm

When a male sperm, or seed, and a female egg join together, the egg is fertilized. It becomes the first cell of a brand new person.

Everybody, no matter who they are, or where they come from, starts life in the same way.

Beginning with a single cell, it takes about 40 weeks for a baby to grow inside its mother. It lives and develops inside the womb, which protects the baby until it's ready to be born.

THE WOMB
The womb, or uterus, is an amazing organ. It sits in the abdomen and is normally about the size of a chicken's egg. However, as a baby begins to grow, so does the womb. It gradually stretches to makes a safe, comfortable home for the baby, right up until it's ready to be born. By then, an average baby weighs about 3.2 kg (7 lbs) and measures 35–50 cm (13–20 inches) long – much bigger than a chicken's egg! Sometimes, babies are born too early. It's a lot harder for them to survive and carry on growing in the outside world than it is inside the womb.

A fertilized egg is called a zygote. It then becomes an embryo and, after 8 weeks, a fetus (or foetus).

5 days   21 days   28 days   48 days   56 days   12 weeks   16 weeks   6 months   8 months

GROWING CELLS

Once an egg has been fertilized, it moves along the fallopian tube and into the womb. There, it starts to divide. First, it splits in half, so one cell becomes two. Those two cells split in half, to make four, and these then divide and make eight. The cells keep splitting until there are billions of them. They then begin to move around and arrange themselves in the right place, as they grow into a baby.

Inside the womb, a baby is joined to its mother by the umbilical cord. This provides oxygen and nutrients to help it grow.

Genes in our cells, contain the information needed to build a new person and new cells. They're made from a material called DNA.

SCAN

Doctors can look at a baby inside the womb using sound-waves and echoes. A computer turns the sound into pictures, so the doctor can see the baby and make sure it's growing properly.

Scan of a baby inside the womb

Amniotic fluid

Umbilical cord

Placenta

Muscle (rectus abdominis)

Womb (uterus)

Fetus

Cervix

Birth canal

GROWTH AND ENERGY

A special group of organs takes care of our moods, energy and growth.

These organs, or glands, make up what is known as the endocrine system. They work together to control all sorts of things, from how tall we grow to what time we wake up in the morning.

ENDOCRINE SYSTEM

The glands in the endocrine system come in different shapes and sizes. Each gland is made from a group of cells that produces a particular type of chemical. These chemicals are called hormones. Glands release the hormones straight into the bloodstream. Blood then transports them, like chemical messages, to other cells around the body.

HORMONES

Hormones are chemicals that make cells behave in a certain way. There are over 30 types of hormone in the human body and they each have a different job to do. Each endocrine gland releases exactly the right amount of hormones, at exactly the right time.

The pituitary gland is only the size of a pea, but it is in charge of the whole endocrine system. It also makes growth hormones. The nearby pineal gland controls sleep patterns.

Pituitary gland

Pineal gland

The thyroid is a butterfly-shaped gland in the neck. It makes hormones that control how fast the cells in our body use up energy.

DID YOU KNOW?

Adrenaline, from the adrenal glands, is sometimes called the 'fight, or flight' hormone. It helped our ancestors run away from predators, or stand up to them.

The pancreas is the biggest endocrine gland. It produces a hormone called insulin, which lets cells make energy from sugar in the bloodstream.

DIABETES AND INSULIN

Diabetes is an illness that happens when the pancreas doesn't make enough insulin. Without insulin, our cells can't absorb, or use up sugar. The sugar stays in the bloodstream and can make us very unwell.

Fruit contains sugar

Testes produce male hormones known as androgens. These let boys' bodies know when to start making changes, such as growing facial hair, during puberty.

FEMALE OVARIES

Female ovaries

A girl's ovaries make eggs and female hormones, called oestrogen and progesterone. Just like testes for boys, they let a girl's body know when to start going through puberty. They also prepare the body for having babies later in life.

Thymus hormones teach the body how to fight germs and disease. Once you're grown up, its job is done and the thymus shrinks away to almost nothing.

Adrenal glands release hormones that help the body to cope with difficult, or dangerous situations. You can sometimes feel them working when you get 'butterflies' in your stomach.

GETTING OLDER

All the time we are growing up, our body is busy changing. But it doesn't stop changing once we're an adult!

Many changes happen as we grow old. Hair turns silver and wrinkles appear on skin. Everyone ages, and, just like getting taller, or losing baby teeth, it's a completely natural process.

AGEING

The body is made from billions of cells. Some of them last for a very long time, but many need to be replaced more regularly. To do this, cells multiply by splitting themselves in half. But they can only do this so many times before they die. As we get older, more and more cells are lost, or damaged, and the body finds it harder to replace them. Without the new cells, muscles become weaker, organs don't work as well and the immune system finds it harder to fight off infections and disease.

When you're young, the immune system heals cuts and broken bones around five times faster than it can by the time you're sixty.

Puberty happens during your teenage years. You start changing from a child into an adult, growing faster than any time since you were a baby. It usually finishes before you reach your twenties.

NEW BORN

Newborn babies grow very quickly and need lots of sleep to do this. Most of us double in length and grow three times heavier during our first year.

New born baby

WRINKLES AND AGE SPOTS

As we age, the cells that make skin stretchy and elastic start to disappear. The layer of fat underneath vanishes, so the skin isn't plumped out any more and it forms into wrinkles. Some people also get age spots – dark patches caused by melanin in the skin.

Over many years, our bones gradually become thinner, weaker and more easily broken. This can cause some people to stoop, or even to shrink in height. Changes to bones in the middle ear can also cause hearing problems for older people.

Weaker bones can be painful

DID YOU KNOW?

All our muscles grow weaker with age, including those in the eyes. This causes many people to become long-sighted, but the problem can easily be fixed by wearing glasses.

From your mid-twenties, you slowly start to lose nerve cells. This means you might do some things a bit more slowly. Now you've stopped growing, you also need less sleep.

In middle age, people often start to get wrinkles and silver hairs. These changes start sooner in some people than others – there's no set age when they happen.

As we get older, the cells that make our hair brown, black, or red start to die off, leaving it white or silver.

WHEEZES, DISEASES AND HEALING

The immune system is made up of chemicals, tissues and organs. When it senses an infection, it makes new chemicals, called antibodies, to protect the body.

Immune (or lymph) system

Lymph nodes are part of the immune system. They are clusters of disease-fighting cells that trap germs. When they're battling an infection, they swell up. You can sometimes feel them as bean-shaped lumps in your neck when you're ill.

Lymph node

Our body's built-in healing system fights off illness and helps to repair injuries.

Every day, different parts of the body work hard to protect us from thousands of germs and infections. But, everyone is ill from time to time. Luckily, when that happens, our immune system is there to help us get better as quickly as possible.

WHY DO WE GET ILL?

Most illnesses are caused by germs inside our bodies that shouldn't be there. When the germs get in, they make themselves at home, using up the energy and nutrients we need to stay healthy. They sometimes produce a kind of poison, too. Some of the symptoms we suffer might also be caused by our immune system trying to destroy the germs.

DID YOU KNOW?

Allergies happen when the immune system mistakes harmless things, such as pollen, for dangerous germs. It attacks them with chemicals that can make us sneeze.

GERMS

If a germ makes it into your body, you won't necessarily become ill. You might have built up an immunity to certain types of germs. This means the germ can't survive in your body. It usually happens when you've had a disease once before. Your immune system works hard to get rid of the germs, so when the same type attack again, it remembers how to fight them off. The germs are quickly destroyed before they can spread and cause infection.

Colds are caused by viruses. We catch them more often than any other disease, sometimes up to 12 times a year.

Flu (also caused by a virus) is more serious than a cold and often causes the body's temperature to rise. Heating the body is another way in which the immune system fights infection.

VACCINATIONS

Vaccinations trick your body into protecting itself. Doctors inject you with a harmless version of the germ that causes a disease and your immune system learns how to fight it, in case you catch the real thing.

A doctor uses a stethoscope to listen to the sounds that a patient's body is making. Wheezing can be a sign that the immune system is fighting an infection.

RECORD-BREAKING FACTS AND FIGURES

From the smallest organ to the biggest bone, the whole body is amazing.

We have hundreds of muscles, billions of brain cells and more than 100,000 km (60,000 miles) of blood vessels, but which bits of us are the real record breakers?

HAIR RECORDS

The fastest-growing part of the body is bone marrow, but hair comes a close second. Beard hairs are the speediest growers of all. Without shaving, a man could grow a 9 m (30 ft) beard over the course of his life.

People with blonde hair usually have the highest number of hairs on their head (about 130,000). Redheads have the fewest, with 80,000 to 90,000.

The least-hairy areas of the body are the palms of our hands and the soles of our feet. These are the only two areas where we have no hair follicles at all.

The liver is the largest and heaviest of our internal organs.

The pineal gland is the smallest organ in the body.

The biggest artery in the body is the aorta. It's about the same thickness as a garden hose!

The body's largest muscle is the gluteus maximus in our buttocks.

The longest human tongue ever recorded was over 9.5 cm (3.7 inches) in length.

DID YOU KNOW?

Human beings have the most complicated brain in the world. Almost all scientists believe it's the most complicated organ in the body.

LONG IN THE LEG

Tooth enamel is the hardest substance in the human body.

DID YOU KNOW?

We have seven vertebrae (bones) in our neck – exactly the same number as a giraffe! The giraffe's bones are just much, much longer than ours.

Our legs are multiple record breakers! The femur, or thighbone, is the longest bone in the body and the sartorius, which is also in the thigh, is the longest muscle. Running from the lower back down the whole length of the leg, the sciatic nerve is the body's longest and widest nerve.

The smallest muscle in the body is found in the ear. The stapedius is just over 1 mm (0.04 inch) long.

Blood supplies every part of the body except for the cornea and lens in the eye (and a few other obscure parts).

The nail on the middle finger grows faster than any of the others. The thumbnail is the slowest grower.

TALLER, SHORTER

It might sound strange, but we're taller first thing in the morning than we are by the end of the day! Discs of cartilage between the bones in our spine get squashed and flattened by gravity during the daytime. This makes our spine a little bit shorter. While we're lying down asleep, the discs go back to normal and our full height is restored.

GLOSSARY

Abdomen Part of the body between the chest and hipbone containing the stomach and major organs.

Bloodstream The flow of blood around the body.

Cardiovascular Relating to the heart and blood vessels (also known as the circulatory system).

Cartilage Strong, but flexible material found in areas of the body including the ears, nose, knees and joints.

Cavity A hole, or hollow space.

Cell The smallest unit of life – all living things are made up of cells.

Cuticle A thin, u-shaped piece of skin at the base of finger and toenails.

Dentin Tough, bone-like material that makes up part of a tooth.

DNA A chemical in every cell that controls the cell's shape, purpose and the way it behaves.

Epiglottis A flap of tissue at the bottom of the tongue that stops food going into the windpipe.

Evaporate, evaporation A process in which a liquid, such as water, is turned into a gas by heating it.

External On the outside of the body.

Fallopian tubes Two tubes that connect the ovaries to the womb in females.

Germ A tiny, single-cell life-form that often spreads disease.

Gland An organ that makes a particular chemical, or substance to be released inside, or outside the body. Hormones and sweat are made by glands.

Haversian system (osteon) Tiny, tube-shaped bundles of tissue that make up compact bone.

Immune Protected against, or not at risk from, a particular type of germ, or a disease, such as measles.

Infection A disease caused by a germ that gets inside the body and begins to multiply.

Internal On the inside of the body.

Involuntary An action that takes place without us choosing, or deciding to do it.

Keratin A tough chemical substance and the main element in our hair and nails.

Long-sighted A problem with the eyes that stops a person seeing an object clearly if the object is too close to them.

Melanin A pigment found in hair, skin and eyes. One type of melanin causes red hair and freckles.

Nucleus The part of a cell that controls the rest of the cell.

Nutrients Chemicals, often obtained from food, that a plant, or animal needs in order to live and grow.

Olfactory Relating to smells, or the sense of smell.

Organ A part of the body that has a particular job to do. Ears are external organs and the heart, lungs and kidneys are internal organs.

Oxygen A clear gas that makes up about one fifth of the air we breathe and is essential to all living things.

Particle A tiny piece of matter, or substance.

Pigment A substance that makes, or gives something a particular hue, such as green, or blue.

Puberty The process during which a child turns into an adult.

Saliva A watery substance made in the mouth, also known as spit.

Sensory Linked to the senses (sight, hearing, smell, taste and touch).

Sign language A communication system that uses hand-gestures and signals instead of speech.

Skeletal Relating to the skeleton, or the bones of the skeleton.

Tissue Part of the body, or an organ, made from a group of cells that look the same and do the same thing.

Vaccination To inject someone with a vaccine – a substance that makes the immune system fight against a particular disease.

Vibrations, vibrate Small, fast, shaking movements that are often felt, rather than seen.

Voicebox The organ that makes sounds as you talk or sing, and also controls the volume.

Voluntary An action that you willingly choose or decide to perform.

INDEX